Face to Face

WHALES

Q2AMedia

Created by Q2A Media
www.q2amedia.com
Text, design & illustrations Copyright © 2008 Q2AMedia

Editor Jean Coppendale
Publishing Director Chester Fisher
Creative Director Simmi Sikka
Art Director Joita Das
Senior Designers Ritu Chopra and Neha Kaul
Project Manager Hemant Sharma

Illustrators Subhash Vohra and Aadil A Siddiqui
Art Editor Akansha Srivastava
Picture Researcher Debabrata Sen

an imprint of
■SCHOLASTIC
www.scholastic.com

Published by Tangerine Press, an imprint of Scholastic Inc., 557 Broadway; New York, NY 10012

Scholastic Canada Ltd.; Markham, Ontario

Scholastic Australia Pty. Ltd; Gosford NSW

Scholastic New Zealand Ltd.; Greenmount, Auckland

10 9 8 7 6 5 4 3 2 1

ISBN: 978-0-545-27401-2

Printed in Shenzhen, China

Picture Credits

t = top, b = bottom, c = center, r = right, l = left

Cover Image: Q2A Media Artwork.
Back: Istock.
Full title: Howard Hall/Photolibrary.
Imprint: Christian Musat/Shutterstock.
Half title: Gerard Soury/Photolibrary.
Content images: Kelvin Aitken/ Photolibrary; Kevin Schafer/Photolibrary.

6 David Fleetham/Ecoscene; **6-7** Mark Carwardine/Photolibrary; **7** Gerard Soury/Photolibrary; **8** Gerard Soury/ Photolibrary; **8-9** North Wind Pictures/ Photolibrary; **10** oriontrail/Shutterstock; **10t** Watt Jim/Photolibrary; **10b** Kevin Schafer/Photolibrary; **11** AlaskaStock/ Photolibrary; **12** Phillip Colla/Ecoscene;

12-13 Norbert Wu/Minden Pictures/ National Geographic Stock; **14** Andrey Nekasov/Ecoscene; **16t** François Gohier/ Ecoscene; **16b** Armin May Forest/ Photolibrary; **17** Paul Nicklen/National Geographic Stock; **16-17** Baloncici/ Shutterstock; **19** Rosemary Calvert/ Photolibrary; **20** Howard Hall/Photolibrary; **21t** Kelvin Aitken/Photolibrary; **21b** Stephan Kerkhofs/Shutterstock; **22t** Jonathan Hayway/Associated Press; **22b** Rich Carey/Shutterstock; **24l** Gerard Soury/Photolibrary; **24r** Istock; **25** Eric Cheng/Barcroft Media; **26-27** Chris Cheadle/Photolibrary; **27** Flip Nicklin/ Minden Pictures/National Geographic Stock; **28** Perrine Doug/Photolibrary; **28-29** Razvan Stroie/Shutterstock; **29l** Bartlomiej Stroinski/Shutterstock; **29r** Chee-Onn Leong/Shutterstock; **30** François

Gohier/Ecoscene; **32** Kelvin Aitken/ Photolibrary; **32-33** Duncan Murrell/ Photolibrary; **34-35** Steven Kazlowski/ Ecoscene; **35** Kelvin Aitken/Photolibrary; **36** David B Fleetham/Photolibrary; **36-37** Razvan Stroie/Shutterstock; **37** Kelvin Aitken/Photolibrary; **38l** Richard Fitzer/ Shutterstock; **38r** François Gohier/ Ecoscene; **39** Brett Atkins/Shutterstock; **40** O. Louis Mazzatenta/National Geographic Stock; **40-41** Razvan Stroie/Shutterstock; **41** Flip Nicklin/Minden Pictures/National Geographic Stock; **42t** Sutton-Hibbert/Rex Features; **42b** Howard Hall/Photolibrary; **43** David Fleetham/Ecoscene; **44-45** Robinson Ed/Photolibrary; **46-47** Chris Cheadle/ Photolibrary; **48** Rich Carey/Shutterstock.

Q2AMedia Art Bank: 15, 18, 23, 31.

WHALES

Sally Morgan

an imprint of
■SCHOLASTIC
www.scholastic.com

Contents

Ocean Giants

Whales are the giants of the oceans, and the blue whale is the largest animal ever to have lived on Earth. The blue whale is bigger than any of the dinosaurs.

tail flukes

Large and small

The blue whale grows up to 100 feet (30 m) long and weighs as much as 180 tons (163 tonnes). That's about the same as 20 African elephants! The smallest whales are the pygmy and dwarf sperm whales that are 8 to 12 feet (2.5 to 3.8 m) long.

Fish or mammal?

Whales may look like giant fish, but they are **mammals**. A whale has a tail that ends in a pair of horizontal, rubbery lobes called **flukes**, whereas the tail of a fish ends in a vertical fin. Whales breathe air, and females give birth to live young and produce milk to feed them.

A playful killer whale at sunset.

Most mammals have a covering of hair over the body but whales have a few **bristles**, mostly on their head.

FACT

▶❘ *For hundreds of years, people knew very little about whales. All they saw was the odd glimpse of a head or tail.*

blow hole

head

flipper

mouth

Whales spend their entire lives underwater. They even give birth to their calves in water! This is unlike other marine mammals, such as seals, that have to come ashore to give birth.

▲ *The blue whale is as long as three school buses and its heart is the size of a car.*

Cetaceans

There are about 4,600 different species of mammals, which are subdivided into smaller groups. The members of each group have certain features in common. Whales belong to the group of mammals called **cetaceans** (si-TEY-shuhns). There are close to 90 species of cetaceans, which include dolphins and porpoises, as well as whales.

This short-finned pilot whale is a common whale frequently seen around boats.

Whales and people

The Inuit people of the Arctic relied on bowhead whales for oil and meat. Once the whale was killed, they used all of its body, wasting nothing. During the nineteenth century, European whalers killed millions of whales for their oil, meat, and whalebone. Whales were very valuable. A single bowhead whale could fetch $8,000, a huge sum of money in those days. Today, most people prefer to watch whales rather than hunt them.

▼ An artist's rendition of a whale hunt in the nineteenth century. The whale is surrounded by a number of small boats carrying people armed with harpoons.

FACT

The book *Moby Dick* by Herman Melville is the story of a huge sperm whale named Moby Dick that sinks Captain Ahab's boat. Ahab becomes obsessed with the whale and hunts Moby Dick but is drowned when the rope of his **harpoon** is caught around him and the whale drags him underwater.

Living Underwater

Whales have a smooth, **streamlined** body that enables them to glide through the oceans.

Flippers and fins

Whales' flippers are paddle-like and help the whale to steer. The dorsal fin on their back helps keep their body upright in the water. The tail is powerful and ends with a large fluke that pushes the whale through the water.

tail fluke

▶| *The up and down movement of the tail pushes the whale through the water.*

☒ *The whale has a body that narrows toward the tail.*

Diving deep

To dive deep, a whale does a "headstand" on the surface of the water. It arches its back so its head dives into the water and the tail pops out. With a beat of its tail, it disappears below the surface. Most whales dive to depths of 320 feet to 650 feet (100 m to 200 m). The killer whale only dives to about 98 feet (30 m).

The beaked whale is a real diving expert. It can dive to depths of 6,230 feet (1,900 m), which is even deeper than the dives of the sperm whale.

FACT

The whale uses its powerful tail to dive deep into the ocean.

Blubber

Oceans are cold places, especially in the Arctic and Antarctic, so whales have a thick layer of fat, or **blubber**, under their skin. The blubber helps trap heat in the body, so the whale stays warm in cold water.

◄ *The two blowholes of the humpback whale.*

▲ *When a whale surfaces, it opens its blowhole and a jet of air and water from its lungs explodes into the air. Then, it takes another breath.*

Holding their breath

A whale may look like a fish, but it does not breathe in the same way. Fish have gills, but whales have lungs, just like people. A whale breathes through nostrils, called a **blowhole**, on top of its head. Toothed whales have a single blowhole, while baleen whales have two. Whales have to come to the surface to breathe.

People can hold their breath underwater for a few minutes, but most whales can stay underwater for 10 to 20 minutes. The record holder is the sperm whale, which can hold its breath for up to 90 minutes, so it can dive deep to search for food.

FACT

When whales surface, the blowout of water and air through their blowholes may reach more than 45 feet (15 m) into the air.

The Whale Family

Whales are divided into two groups according to whether they have teeth or not. The two groups are the toothed whales and the baleen whales.

Toothed whales

The toothed whales, as their name suggests, have small, pointed teeth. The largest toothed whale is the sperm whale, which can grow to almost 60 feet (18 m) in length. The best known is probably the killer whale, or orca, with its distinctive black and white colors. Other toothed whales include the white whales (narwhal and beluga), pilot, and beaked whales. Toothed whales have a swelling on their forehead, known as a melon. This is filled with a liquid and used in **echolocation**, an ability to detect objects in the water using sound. The melon of the sperm whale is particularly large. In front of the melon of some toothed whales is a beak.

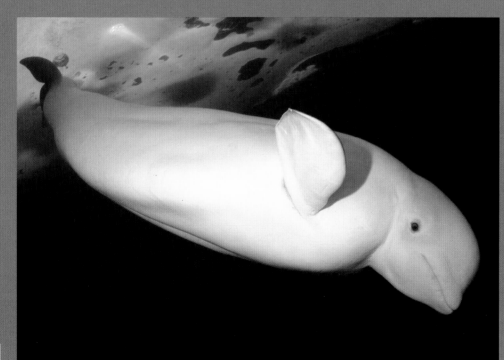

◀ *The beluga is the only all-white whale, a color that blends well with the ice of the Arctic.*

blowhole

eye patch

When they are hunting, killer whales can dive to a depth of 98 feet (30 m).

Dorsal fins in males reach a height of 6 feet (1.8 m).

Killer whales have 10 to 14 teeth on each side of the jaw.

Killer whales have a total of 40–56 teeth. The largest are about 4 inches (10 cm) long.

Killer whales are easily identified by their black and white markings. They are expert hunters with sleek bodies and powerful tails.

FACT

Male beaked whales have two cone-shaped teeth that stick out like tusks.

Baleen whales

The baleen whales do not have teeth. Instead, they have two rows of long **baleen plates** hanging from their upper jaw. These comb-like plates are made from baleen, which is the same substance that forms claws and nails. Some baleen whales have throat pleats, or grooves, so their throat can expand as they take in mouthfuls of water.

The tiny bristles on the baleen plates trap food.

The bowhead whale has an extra-large head with a curved jaw to accommodate the long baleen plates.

Barnacles

Many baleen whales have barnacles growing on their body. The barnacles do not harm the whale. As the whale swims, the **barnacles** feed on **plankton** (microscopic plant and animal life) in the water.

The southern right whale has about 25 throat pleats. These open up when the whale feeds and allow the whale to take a huge gulp of water and food. The water is then filtered out through the whale's baleen plates.

FACT

The bowhead whale has approximately 340 plates attached to its upper jaw. Some of the plates are up to 15 feet (4.6 m) long.

Watery World

Whales are found in all the world's oceans, especially in the cold waters of the Arctic and Antarctic. They are found at the surface as well as in the deep ocean.

The tusk is a tooth that grows into a long spiral up to 10 feet (3 m) long. The tusk can weigh up to 22 lbs. (10 kg).

The narwhal sucks fish and mollusks into its mouth.

The skin becomes paler with age.

The body is about 13 to 16 feet (4 to 5 m) long.

▷ *The male narwhal usually has only one tooth, which grows through the upper lip. The females are usually toothless. Males are often seen "fencing" with each other using their tusks.*

Cold water whales

Cold water is rich in plankton and **krill**. The abundance of food brings whales to the polar seas. The bowhead, beluga, and narwhal spend their lives in the Arctic Ocean, where they live among the ice floes.

In summer, minke whales are seen in the icy waters around Antarctica where there is plenty of food such as plankton, krill, and fish.

Polar summer

Other whales, such as gray and fin whales, can be found in the Arctic Ocean during the summer months. Many whales, including the humpback, blue, fin, sperm, minke, and killer whales, also visit the Southern Ocean around the Antarctic in search of food.

Into the deep

Some whales dive deep in the ocean in search of food. Only the surface layer of the water, to depths of 650 feet (200 m), is lit by the Sun. Below this, there is just enough light to allow whales to find their prey. At 3,280 feet (1,000 m), it is pitch black. Sperm and beaked whales dive into this zone to find food.

FACT

Sperm whales can stay underwater for at least an hour. They can dive to depths greater than 3,900 feet (1,200 m). They dive quickly, too, at 550 feet (170 m) per minute.

Gray whales

Gray whales spend the summer months feeding in the Arctic Ocean. Then, they swim south in small groups of about 10 to the warm waters off the coast of the U.S. and Mexico, where the females give birth. This journey takes from two to three months. Once the winter is over, the whales and their calves swim back to the Arctic.

◄ *Gray whales are bottom feeders. They lie on their side and take huge mouthfuls of mud and water, which they filter through their baleen plates.*

Gray whales have lots of barnacles on one side of their body, but none on the other. This is because the whale always lies on the same side to feed, so the barnacles get scraped off.

In May 2010, there was a confirmed sighting of a gray whale off the coast of Israel in the Mediterranean Sea. Some scientists believe the whales may be repopulating old breeding grounds that have not been used for centuries.

Long journeys

The minke whale, like the one pictured, normally does not migrate but is found around the world, from the polar seas to the equator. Many of the larger whales make long **migrations** each year. Whales such as the blue, humpback, fin, and gray swim between their feeding grounds in the cold oceans to warmer waters near the equator, where they breed.

dorsal fin is sickle shaped

distinctive gray marks along the sides of the body

When resting, the minke whale stays near the surface, spouting 5 to 6 times a minute.

pointed flipper with white band

narrow, v-shaped head with pointed snout and large mouth

The minke is a small baleen whale and is found in the surface waters of all the world's oceans. It travels alone, or in small pods of 2 to 3 individuals.

Life Cycle

Whales give birth to a single baby called a calf. Twin whale calves are very rare. Usually, when a female gives birth to twins, just one survives.

Giving birth

Most female whales are **pregnant** for about a year, but a female killer whale is pregnant for 17 months. Many female whales swim to special places to give birth where there is a good supply of food and few predators. For example, California gray whales give birth in the shallow waters off the coast of Mexico.

Qila, a beluga whale at the Vancouver Aquarium in Canada, gives birth to a calf in captivity. The mother whale was in labor for nearly three hours.

First moments

Usually a whale calf is born tail first, but some are born headfirst. Whales cannot breathe underwater, so the newborn whale knows **instinctively** that it must get to the surface within a few seconds or it will drown. It wiggles its tail, and its mother nudges it with her flippers toward the surface, where it takes its first breath of air. Within 30 minutes or so, the newborn whale calf is ready to swim with its mother.

calf uses its flippers to balance in the water

calf beats its tail to swim to the surface

The calf has to take its first breath within 10 seconds or so of its birth.

This humpback mother and calf may stay together for a year or more and develop a very strong bond.

FACT

A newborn blue whale calf is more than 22 feet (7 m) long and weighs about 6.6 tons (6 tonnes).

First lessons

A newborn whale calf has a lot to learn in the first few minutes of its life. First, it has to learn to breathe through its blowhole without swallowing water. Then, it has to learn how to swim without rolling around in the water.

The mother stays close to her calf, to protect it and to direct its movement.

Killer whales are playful animals, especially the calves, which are often seen leaping out of the water.

FACT

As many as half of all killer whale calves die within the first six months of life. Scientists are not sure why so many die. Some may be killed by other predators, such as sharks, and others die from disease.

Rich milk

A mother whale's milk is very rich in fat. The fat makes the milk very thick, like cream. This means that the milk does not **dissolve** easily in the water. The fatty milk helps the calf grow quickly and produce a thick layer of blubber so that it stays warm in the water.

A sperm whale calf drinks about 35 pints (20 l) of its mother's milk a day. This increases to as much as 350 pints (616 l) as it grows older.

▶▶ *This sperm whale calf is feeding on its mother's milk.*

Growing up

Most calves feed on their mother's milk for about a year. Once they are **weaned** and no longer rely on their mother for food, they swim off to live on their own or with other whales. Some, such as female killer whale calves, stay with their mother for life.

Living together

Most whales live in small groups called **pods**. Some pods are formed from just females and their young, but others are family groups. Scientists think killer whales like to socialize with each other. Pods come together for just a few hours to form super-pods of 100 or more killer whales. This allows them to mix with whales from other pods.

Humpback pods

Humpback whales live in small pods of 2 to 15 individuals. Unlike the killer whale pods, the humpback pods are short-lived. Individuals come together for a few days or weeks and then split up. Females stay with their calves for about a year. During this time, they are joined by another adult that acts as an **escort**. The escort is usually a male.

▼ A pod of killer whales off the coast of Canada. Male killer whales are found at the edge of the pod and the calves are in the middle.

Killer whale pods

Killer whales live in pods of 5 to 30 individuals. The pod is made up of a family group of males and females with calves that is led by a female whale. Killer whales have long lives so there may be as many as four **generations** living together in a pod.

Calf nursery

Sperm whales live in pods of females and their calves. Young calves cannot dive to great depths, so they cannot follow their mother when she dives to find food. Instead, the young calves stay together at the surface guarded by the other females.

◄ *A pod of sperm whales swimming with a baby.*

27

Senses

Whales rely on their senses to find their way around the ocean and to locate food.

Sight and sound

Whales have small eyes for their size. Most whales can see well, but sight is of little use in dark or murky water, so they rely on their other senses. In water, sounds travel fast over long distances, so whales have a well-developed sense of hearing.

Underwater, whales can only see about 35 feet (10.7 m) in front of them.

FACT

The skin of a whale is rich in blood vessels and nerves, and is very sensitive to touch.

Echolocation

Sound is especially important to toothed whales, such as killer whales, as they use it to locate prey. This is called echolocation. It's like SONAR used by submarines. These whales produce a series of very high-pitched clicks. The beam of sound travels through the water in front of the whale and bounces off a nearby object. This produces an echo that the whale can hear. The whale figures out the position of the object from the time it takes for the echo to return.

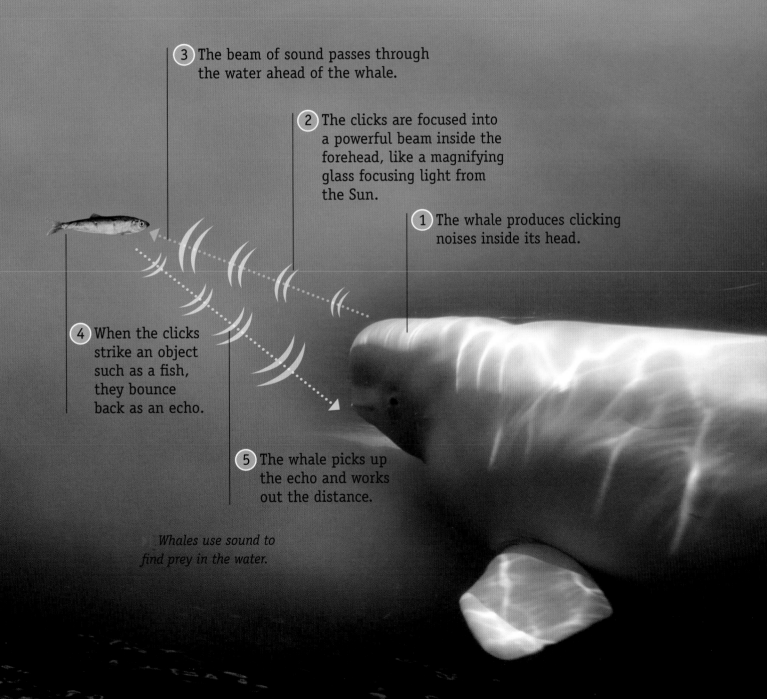

3 The beam of sound passes through the water ahead of the whale.

2 The clicks are focused into a powerful beam inside the forehead, like a magnifying glass focusing light from the Sun.

1 The whale produces clicking noises inside its head.

4 When the clicks strike an object such as a fish, they bounce back as an echo.

5 The whale picks up the echo and works out the distance.

Whales use sound to find prey in the water.

Whale **Food**

Whales feed on a range of different animals such as fish, squid, and seals. Surprisingly, the largest whales feed on some of the ocean's smallest animals!

Toothed hunters

Toothed whales hunt mostly for fish and squid, but they may catch seals, sea birds, and even giant squid. Their pointed teeth are perfect for catching slippery fish. They swallow prey whole or break it into chunks. Often, toothed whales swim at full speed into a **shoal** of fish so the fish become confused and are easier to catch.

One of the fiercest predators in the sea is the killer whale. Killer whales hunt together and are often nicknamed the "wolves of the sea" because they behave like a pack of wolves. They chase and catch fish, seals, and sea lions. They even attack sharks and the calves of other whales.

In South America, some killer whales have learned how to swim into the shallows to catch seals in the surf.

Battles in the deep

Sperm whales are hungry whales. They need to eat about three percent of their body weight every day. That's about 2,200 lbs. (1,000 kg) of food a day for an adult male! Their favorite food is squid. Most of the time they feed on medium-sized squid, but sometimes they hunt the giant and colossal squids in the deep ocean.

The large suckers of the squid grip the whale's skin and leave a white scar.

The giant squid has a sharp beak and strong arms covered in large suckers.

Sperm whales sometimes dive down to 3,000 feet (900 m) to hunt giant squid, which live in the deep, dark oceans.

The whale's pointed teeth are perfect for gripping slippery prey.

The whale grips its prey in its huge jaws.

⊼ *The fin whale is a gulper. It swims at high speed at swarms of krill, opens its mouth, and takes a mouthful of water and food.*

FACT

The fin whale can gulp a volume of water that is the size of a school bus— that's a huge mouthful! Each mouthful may contain up to 26 lbs. (12 kg) of food.

Filter feeders

Baleen whales strain, or filter, food from the water using their baleen plates that hang from their upper jaw. Some baleen whales gulp huge mouthfuls of water, while others swim along with their mouths open.

Gulpers

Whales such as the blue, fin, and humpback are gulpers. This means they take huge mouthfuls of seawater containing food and then use their massive tongue to force the water through the plates, where the bristles trap tiny animals.

⊻ *The pleats on the throat allow baleen whales to expand their throats to swallow more food.*

Skimmers

Some baleen whales are skimmers. These whales, such as the right and bowhead whales, catch food by swimming with their mouths open. Water enters the mouth and passes through the plates, which traps the food. Usually, they skim the water near the surface, but they will also skim along the seabed, trapping crabs and flat fish.

Bubble nets

The humpback whale has a clever way of catching prey. It swims around a shoal of fish or a swarm of krill, blowing bubbles to create a spectacular wall of bubbles that stops the prey from escaping. Then the whale charges up through the shoal from below and takes a huge gulp of fish and water. Often, humpback whales work together to create huge bubble nets up to 98 feet (30 m) in diameter to trap large shoals of fish.

▶| *The frothy water around these feeding humpback whales is produced by a bubble net.*

FACT

The tongue of a blue whale weighs more than an Asian elephant!

Krill are crustaceans with many pairs of long feeding legs and five pairs of swimming legs.

Krill

Many baleen whales, especially the blue whale, feed on krill. Krill are tiny, shrimp-like animals that live in large groups called swarms. They are one of the most plentiful animals in the ocean and are the food of many marine animals, such as mackerel, salmon, squid, and seabirds, as well as whales.

Finding food

The filter-feeding whales do not just open their mouths and hope they catch some food. They are hunters and use their senses, especially hearing, to find large swarms of krill or shoals of fish.

Whale Talk

Whales talk to each other in many different ways. Sound is very important for communication because it travels quickly and over great distances in water.

Whistles and squeals

Whales make many different sounds, such as whistles, squeals, moans, and trills. These sounds spread through the water and are heard by other whales. This form of communication is important as the whale pods live in different parts of huge oceans, and it helps them stay in touch.

As well as sound, whales also use touch to communicate.

The moans of the blue whale are the loudest sounds produced by any animal. If you were standing close to a jet engine, its sound would reach around 140 decibels. Blue whales make a sound that is 10,000 times more powerful and loud enough to travel across an ocean.

FACT

Each whale song is made up of up to 7 themes, which are repeated in the same order over and over again.

Whale song

As well as making sounds, the male humpback whale can also sing! The song of the male humpback is a very eerie mix of groans, moans, and squeaks. Each male includes as many as 30 different sounds in his song. A song can last for as long as 30 minutes, and when he gets to the end of his song, he starts over again. Some singing sessions may last many hours.

Humpback whales have a larynx (voice box) but scientists are unsure how they produce the sounds.

◄ *Originally, scientists thought the whale's song was a way for a male to attract a female. But now, they think a male sings to tell other whales, both male and female, that he is in the area.*

Spyhopping

As well as being fun, breaching and lobtailing are ways of communicating. They create loud sounds that can be heard by other whales at great distances. Whales also rise vertically out of the water for minutes at a time to view their surroundings. This behavior is called **spyhopping**.

◄ *The splash from lobtailing creates a loud sound that travels through the water.*

Breaching and lobtailing

When whales come to the surface, they can leap out of the water, spin around, and crash back down again. This behavior is called **breaching**, and it is especially common among young whales. Another common action is called **lobtailing**, which is when a whale sticks its tail out of the water and slams it down on the surface.

⌃ *When whales spyhop, they can see the splashes created by other whales that are breaching and lobtailing.*

Announcements

Often a whale will breach a number of times after joining a pod. Scientists think that breaching may be a form of announcement, or message, telling the other whales, "I am here!" It could also be seen as a warning to others, because breaching makes a loud noise.

To breach, a whale swims straight up to the surface at full speed and shoots out of the water.

The Future of Whales

Three hundred years ago, there were millions of whales swimming in the oceans. Today, that number is much smaller. For example, the number of blue whales has fallen from about 275,000 in the early eighteenth century to fewer than 10,000 today.

Hunted

The dramatic fall in the numbers of whales was due to widespread hunting in the eighteenth and nineteenth centuries. Whales were hunted and killed for their meat, bones, and oil. Whalers used to boil the whale blubber in huge cauldrons to produce oil, which was used as a fuel in lamps. So many whales were killed that some species almost became **extinct**. Until the 1970s, whale oil was also an ingredient in some cosmetics. Fortunately, a decision was made in 1986 by the International Whaling Commission (IWC) to ban commercial **whaling**.

▼ *A harpooner delivers a fatal blow as whalers close in on a captured sperm whale.*

▲ These divers are rescuing a sperm whale that has become entangled in a fishing net.

Nets and noise

Today, many whales die when they become trapped in fishing nets and drown in the water. Some are badly injured by a ship's propellers. The oceans have become much noisier places because there are more ships and underwater equipment. The additional sounds make it more difficult for whales to communicate over long distances. They become confused and make navigation errors. This may lead to whales becoming stranded on beaches or swimming up rivers by mistake.

FACT

The most **endangered** whales are the bowhead, narwhal, and the Western Pacific gray. There are fewer than 120 individuals of each of these left in the oceans. The Pacific gray whale is found along the east coast of Russia, where it is threatened by oil drilling. The death of just a few females could threaten the survival of this species.

There are many people who want whaling to stop completely. Here, a group from Greenpeace is trying to stop the transfer of whales from a Japanese catcher ship to a whaling factory ship.

More whales

The number of whales is starting to increase again—but it's a slow process. Whales take a long time to reach maturity and the females only have one calf every few years.

Lack of food

However, the main threat to the survival of whales comes from overfishing. Whales feed on krill and fish, which are caught in huge numbers by people. Great care has to be taken so people do not overfish the oceans and leave the whales hungry.

The recovery of the California gray whale has been the most successful. It was once considered to be endangered, but its numbers have increased so much that it has been taken off of the **IUCN Red List**.

FACT

Countries such as Iceland and Norway are catching whales again, and there are fears that others will follow. They claim that the number of whales has increased sufficiently for the whales to be hunted for their meat and oil again—so the future of whales remains uncertain.

Whale watching

Fortunately, whales are popular animals and many people enjoy watching them. In areas where there is good whale watching, such as Baja California and Australia, the local people earn money from whale tourism. This encourages everyone to protect the whales.

▶ *Tourists enjoying the amazing sight of a breaching humpback whale.*

Facts and Records

- The fin whale is the second-largest whale at 88 feet (27 m) long.

- The sperm whale has the largest brain in the animal kingdom. It weighs a massive 20 lbs. (9 kg).

- The sound of the blue whale travels for hundreds of miles. If you dive into deep water off Puerto Rico, you might hear a blue whale off the coast of Newfoundland, more than 1,600 miles (2,575 km) away.

- The right whale gets its name because whalers thought it was the right (correct) whale to kill.

- Right whales swim slowly and do not sink when they are harpooned.

- The bowhead whale has the longest baleen plates of any whale, reaching about 15 feet (4.6 m).

- Blue whales may be large, but their throat is small. They cannot swallow anything larger than a beach ball.

- The fin whale uses its powerful tail flukes to defend itself from killer whales and sharks. Early whalers avoided the fin whale because it would smash their small wooden boats to bits with its tail.

- A newborn blue whale calf is the size of a fully-grown hippopotamus. It drinks up to 800 pints (379 l) of milk a day. And it can gain up to 200 lbs. (90 kg) each day.

- Bowhead whales on average can live longer than any other mammal—100 years or more.

- Gray whales were nicknamed "devilfish" by whalers because female gray whales were so protective of their calves that they attacked the whaling boats.

- Sei whales were not hunted until the blue and fin whale numbers fell. Between 1959 and 1971, 106,886 sei whales were killed in the Southern Ocean. Today, the number of sei whales is about 54,000, $\frac{1}{5}$ the number that existed before whaling.

- Female killer whales are pregnant for about 17 months, the longest of any whale.

- Killer whale calves can make sounds within days of birth. But the sounds are more like high-pitched screams that are nothing like the calls of the adults. It takes the calves two months to learn how to produce the correct sounds.

Glossary

baleen plates The name given to the plates that hang from the upper jaw of baleen whales, which filter out krill from the water when the whales are feeding.

barnacles Barnacles are crustaceans, or hard-shelled marine organisms, that attach themselves to whales, where they feed on small particles of food in the water.

blowhole The nostrils of a whale through which it breathes when it comes to the surface. The blowhole is located on the top or back of a whale's head and is covered by a muscular flap when the whale is underwater.

blubber The thick layer of fat under a whale's skin, which helps keep the whale warm in icy seas.

breaching The name given to the jump a whale makes when it leaps headfirst out of the water, spinning and landing back in the water with a huge splash.

bristles Thick, coarse hairs.

cetaceans The group of animals to which whales and dolphins belong.

dissolve To become a solution by melting; for example, sugar becomes a liquid in hot water.

echolocation The method of using sounds and their echoes to find the direction and distance of objects.

endangered When an animal is at risk of becoming extinct.

escort A humpback whale, usually a male, that accompanies a mother whale and her calf in a pod.

extinct When something no longer exists.

fluke The tail fin of a whale.

generation Whales of approximately the same age.

harpoon A spear with a pointed or barbed point used for hunting animals such as whales, seals, and large fish.

instinctively When an animal behaves in a certain way that is not learned but which is inborn to the particular species.

IUCN Red List This stands for the International Union for Conservation of Nature. It is an internationally recognized list of all the animals and plants that are under threat of becoming extinct.

krill Shrimplike animals that are up to 1¾ inches (5 cm) in length. Krill are the main source of food for baleen whales.

lobtailing When a whale slaps the water with its tail.

mammal An animal that breathes air with lungs, has hair, and gives birth to live young. Female mammals produce milk to feed the babies.

migration A regular or seasonal journey made by an animal.

plankton The tiny plants and animals that float near the surface of the oceans that are eaten by some whales and fish.

pod The name given to a group of whales that may live or travel together.

pregnant When a female animal has a baby or babies developing inside her.

shoal A large number of fish swimming together.

spyhopping When a whale pops its head out of the water to look around.

streamlined Having a torpedo-like shape that slices through water easily.

weaned When a young mammal changes from a diet of milk to an adult diet.

whaling The hunting of whales by people.

Index